THE PERFECT

CHRISTMAS PRESENT

Berwick Coates

A Christmas box for all of you

from fifty me's

Published by Berwick Coates
Publishing partner: Paragon Publishing, Rothersthorpe
First published 2011
© Berwick Coates 2011

ISBN 978-1-908341-30-3

Book design, layout and production management by
Into Print
www.intoprint.net
01604 832149

Printed and bound in UK and USA by Lightning Source

Introduction

There are as many dimensions to Christmas as there are people to look at it. It occurred to me to try and convey some of these many dimensions by means of getting inside the minds of fifty different people and trying to guess how each one of them might see it.

Since Christmas has a trick of spawning cards with snappy rhymes (sometimes, alas, dreadful ones too), and Christmas cards accustom us to savour a good joke (again, alas, some dreadful ones too), verse and pictures seemed a neat way of doing it.

The drawings – I don`t think they qualify as 'cartoons' in the usual sense, and I hesitate to claim their status as 'illustrations' – do not necessarily depict what is in the verses (again I hesitate to call them 'poems'); they are more likely to take the train of thought provoked by the verses a step or two further. As I said in the blurb, the verses try to show what *they* might think; the drawings try to show what *you* might think when you read them.

Whatever you choose to call any of it, I hope the whole package provides a little dollop of Christmas cheer. It is recommended to be taken in fairly small doses, after a festive meal, before a fire, and in good company.

Berwick Coates

Contents

The Shepherd

While we wos in the fiwlds one nigh'
Awl seated on the grahnd,
This bloke come dahn from aht the sky
An` spread `is wings arahnd.

'Nah, don`t be frigh`,' `e said. We said,
'You scared us `arf ta deff!'
`E said, 'I`ve gotta bitta noos
`F ya let me draw me breff.

'There`s this kid wot`s bin bawn, ya see.'
We said. 'That`s nuffin odd.'
'E said, 'This one is.' We said, ' `Ow?'
'E said, 'It`s. . . . sort of. . . . God.'

We laughed an` we said, 'Get away!
We`re stayin` where we are.'
`E pointed upwoods in the sky,
An` said, 'Ya see that star?

'Nah follow it as far as tahn,
Ta that pub by the square.
That stable by the public bar –
You`ll find the kid in there.'

'Ah, flap yer wings an` fly away,'
We said. `E said, 'There`s mawer:
You`ll find `im bandaged up in clorth,
An` lyin` in the straw.'

Then – may I never move – we saw
A very funny thing:
Awl these uvver blokes arrived,
An` they awl began ta sing.

Right funny stuff, it was, an` all –
`Bout God . . . . an` peace on earth.
They chorused an` they `armonised
For awl that they was worth.

Then – jus` like that – they awl was gorn.
It didn`t arf sahnd stiwl.
So, sheepish-like – ta coin a phrase –
We trooped orf dahn the `ill.

Well, we couldn`t sit there after that.
I mean ta say, could you?
We went ta look for this `ere kid.
There was nuffin` else ta do.

We fahnd the stable sure enough,
Wiv the star righ` over`ead.
This kid wos lyin` in the straw
Jus` like the angel said.

`E didn`t look like God ta me.
Then `oo am I ta know?
But I`ll tewl ya this – it made a change
From sittin` in the snow.

The Lawyer

May it please you, my lord, there is no case to plead;
　　There is nothing that stands up in court.
Of the eye-witnesses, most of them can`t write or read,
　　While those that can left no report.

A bemused village carpenter, soaks from the bar,
　　A young mother washed out giving birth.
Plus an innkeeper – surly, as innkeepers are –
　　And some shepherds – the thickest on earth.

If they`d stuck to one story it might have made sense.
　　But they bring in the angels as well.
And the heavenly host, and stars over their tents.
　　Why not throw in the Devil and Hell?

Now my learned friend says, 'What about the Wise Men?'
　　What about them? We have no idea.
They just came in from nowhere, and went off again.
　　They left nothing for eye or for ear.

So, my lord, I must urge you to find as I said,
　　And my haste, I admit, is acute.
It is now Christmas Eve, and my children in bed –
　　I must put on my Santa Claus suit.

The Office Reveller

Were y`ever at the Christmas party t`rown the other week?
In a wide acquaintance with such things I`d say it was unique.
Employees of the Firm enjoyed the Evening of the Year,
When the Managing Director pushed the boat out past the pier.

Pink champagne splashed freely as a thunderstorm.
Drink as Much as Possible was soon the party game.
No-one cared when they found it tasted rather warm;
The bubbles and the fizz got up the nostrils just the same.

With a dumping of rules and a jettison of etiquette;
Hair let down and no-one playing hard to get;
Inhibitions melting in the sun of liquor`s glow;
And everybody finds it hard to say a simple 'No'.

Mr. Julian, the boss` son, now thought it was his chance
To lure the Chief Administrator on a desk to dance.
This lubricated lady, over-eager to comply,
Revealed a vista hitherto denied to human eye.

Dear old Ted, from Stores, Supply, and Maintenance,
Grabs his opportunity to make a little plea.
Girl in question says she`s going off to France,
So cannot share his Boxing Day at Warmington-on-Sea.

With a fall of hierarchy and abandonment of protocol;
Worship at the Golden Calf of canapés and alcohol;
Why was he born so beautiful, why was he born at all?
And what piece of luck we had the ground to break our fall.

We had a call from Mr. Raz Mahomed Ali Khan,
Director of our telephonic staff in Pakistan.
He wished us Merry Christmas and persuaded all the Firm
To sign a direct debit for a twenty-five year term.

Maxitrina, learning to be office girl,
Caught her mini-skirt up as she jumped down off a chair.
Postboy Francis, eager to give sex a whirl,
Thought that God had finally responded to his prayer.

While the hands revolved around the clock regardless of infinity,
Every male sweated to assert his masculinity.
God knows what I did, because the memory`s gone black;
Returning after Boxing Day, I found I`d got the sack.

The Chat-Show Host

It's the Christmas Show of the Century,
Which will promise the world to enthral.
Glue yourself to the telly from now until Sunday;
Mankind will be having a ball.

We aim to raise eighty-five million
For the greatest Good Cause of them all –
Just phone your donation to Saving the Geckos.
Our team will accept every call.

Your happy host, Erica Sprodley,
Is over the moon with the show:
'It's kind of like – oh, it's fantastic. It's mega.
It's Something Else – kind of – y'know?

'The world's greatest boffin is coming –
The one who sits in that chair.
Some machine does his talking – you know – Stephen Hawking.
"Black holes," he says, "aren't really there."

'The Pope sends an email to Islam
(You can't get more holy than that).
Cliff Richard is singing the Lord's Prayer in drag,
And Dai Lama drops in for a chat.

'Mick Jagger performs the Messiah;
Madonna reads Shakespeare in bed;
Tommy Cooper is back, with his fez, just like that;
And Elvis returns from the dead.

'Provided your guests are all famous,
You don`t have to care what they say.
So long as you don`t bore the viewers with God,
The sponsors are happy to pay.'

'Just for the viewers, what do you think was your greatest miracle?'

The Child

My Christmases are terrible;
My Grandma tells me so.
Nothing like the Christmases
That she had long ago.

Grown-ups on the telly shows
Get daft about the past,
When snow was falling everywhere
And 'things were made to last'.

Old fogeys sigh and carry on
About the days gone by,
When children 'knew their proper place',
And didn`t think of 'I'.

Now parents spoil us rotten, so
We don`t know money`s worth.
We`re now so greedy we forget
The day of Jesus` birth.

Funny, though, while grown-ups eat
And drink and drive in danger,
We spend hours in school with scissors
Cutting out a manger.

Silly children spend their Christmas
Wanting things too soon;
Grown-ups are so sensible –
They sleep all afternoon.

Kids who want to stay up late
Are told they`re in the way.
It`s grown-ups` turn, they tell us now –
TV till Boxing Day.

And yet, I still like Christmas, so
When I`m a Grandma too,
I hope I sha`n`t forget the nice things
That I think and do.

The Innkeeper

In my trade life`s not easy (and I daresay nor in yours),
Not even when you`ve sacrificed and prayed.
And have you noticed that it never rains but what it pours –
And great Jehovah`s sparing with his aid.

A perfect illustration of this came a month ago,
The week they did the census for the tax.
My place was full to bursting – all sorts – high and low –
Five days and nights with no chance to relax.

Every room and cubby-hole I had was double-booked;
Only standing room in both the bars.
The larder had been stripped of every scrap that could be cooked.
My staff were serving wine in old, cracked jars.

The busiest night of all, when I was rushed right off my feet –
If I hadn`t been so tired I`d have laughed –
This chap came in from Nazareth – straight in – right off the street,
And asked me for a room. Just like that. Daft.

'It`s not for me, you understand,' he said. 'It`s for the missis.
Baby on the way, and pretty near.'
'Come off it, mate,' I said. 'What kind of place do you think this is?
Besides, you`ve picked the worst night of the year.'

'My wife is going to `ave a kid!' he shouted in my face.
'So what?' I said. 'They get born every day.
You can`t expect the world to turn about. In any case,
What makes this one of yours so special, eh?'

He didn't argue – gave a look that struck me as – well – odd.
'We'll use the stable.' 'Be my guest,' I said.
He muttered to himself, 'It won't upset the Son of God.'
I thought, 'Great Moses, this chap's off his head.'

I got on with my work (well, it was nought to do with me),
Until there came this fuss about a star –
A great big, bright one, overhead. They all rushed out to see.
I didn't have a soul in either bar.

They'd soon get cold, I told myself, and they'd come back for more.
But I was wrong. Do you know what they did?
They all squeezed in the stable, and they knelt down in the straw
To get a glimpse of this poor madman's kid.

That wasn't all, cos there I was, all by myself, inside,
And thinking I would shut up for the night.
I heard a sound, looked up, and saw the door was open wide,
And three men stood there. Gave me quite a fright.

They obviously came from some outlandish place out east;
Their dress was odd, their foreign accents queer.
'We've come to see the baby and we want to join the feast.'
Now how the hell did they know he was here?

Now, as I said, I do my job, and mind my business too,
And I don't care if strangers live or die.
But when King Herod's soldiers came and asked me what I knew,
I kept my mouth shut – and I don't know why.

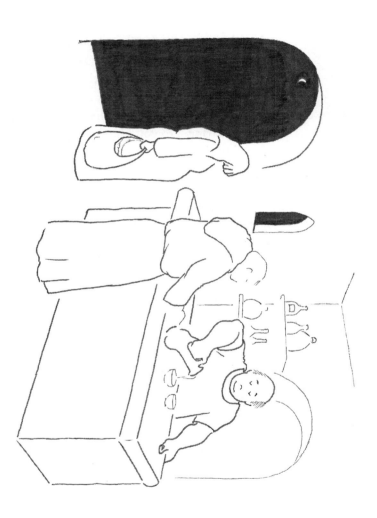

'A baby's only a baby; what's so special about this one?'

The Protester

While the world of the suburbs and red tape conforms,
We meet in our bed-sits and lodgings,
Where we plan to remind that smug world of its sins,
Of its scandals and balls-ups and bodgings.

We draw up a list of our targets and aims,
Of the causes we aim to espouse;
Of the noise we shall make, of the figure we`ll cut –
The attention that we shall arouse.

We`ve come a long way from farm labourers` oaths,
From Chartists` and suffragettes` banners.
It`s mobiles and emails and Internet now,
And i-pods and webcams and scanners.

It`s not the success; it`s the protest that counts.
The fun`s not in winning, but fighting.
Like the General in Gilbert and Sullivan`s song,
Being useless is much more exciting. . . .

Ever since Wat Tyler said the poll tax was iniquitous,
Our strikes and demonstrations have been boringly ubiquitous.
The Internet has millions now of sites on our activities.
The tabloids sell their papers with our scandalous proclivities.

We champion the rights of the vociferous minority.
We are the voice of non-acceptance challenging authority.
We are the true epitome of Britain's protestocracy.
Having bees in bonnets is the soul of our democracy.

But even we can clearly see the need to take a holiday,
And tell our precious consciences it's time to have a jolly day.
On Christmas Day we put away our individuality,
And wallow in a world of unashamed conventionality.

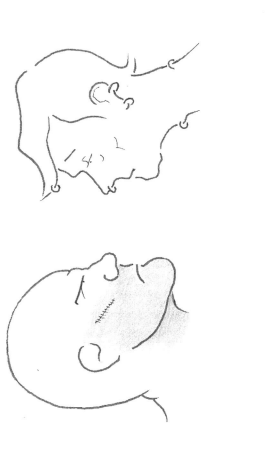

'What are you protesting about?'
'I'm protesting about our right to stop idiots like you protesting.'

Father Christmas

People think they know about my Christmas:
I dedicate it all to girls and boys –
The effort I`ve expended,
The chimneys I`ve descended
To share around the world a billion toys.

My reindeer circumnavigate the planet
At speeds far in excess of sound or light.
I carry out this mission
With the utmost expedition,
And pack it all into a single night.

Everyone just takes it all for granted –
Just hang your stocking up on Christmas Eve.
Say 'Santa, please' politely,
A list of wants each nightly,
Though very few say 'Thanks' when they receive.

By then I never mind `cos I`ve stopped working.
I park my sledge at dawn on Christmas Day.
The reindeer shed their traces.
I leave for warmer places;
When Santa stops his work, he goes to play.

My feet up on a private tropic island.
No nauseating jingle bells to hear.
Unending sun and sand,
A slave or two on hand,
That`s *my* idea of Merry Christmas cheer.

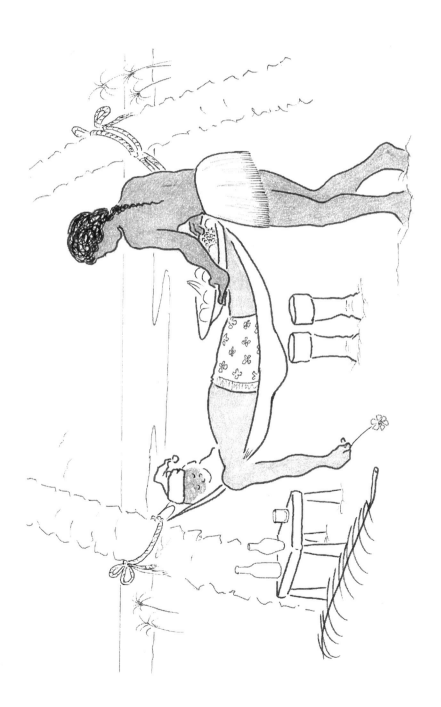

The Celebrity

Just being here, it's fab; it's great.
I watch your show each week.
'What's best about it?' Yeah – well, no;
It's sort of, so to speak.

'That premiere I went to see?'
Of course it was, I think.
Yeah – no. Well, kind of; p'r'aps I'd had
A bit too much to drink.

'The week before?' I did this dance;
I climbed up on the bar.
That writer at the party said
I was a rising star.

I'm booked to do three sessions soon.
I'll go right to the top.
'Barack Obama?' Yeah – well, no –
I don't dig Irish pop.

I like your sofa; it's so soft.
Can I sit this way, please?
So if I hitch it up a bit,
Can they all see my knees?

'Quiz shows?' Yes, I did one once.
I thought it was too square.
If you don't have no GOC's,
The questions are unfair.

'At Christmas?' Yes, I`m sponsored for
The Step-Dad Orphans` scheme.
We must stay drunk for ninety hours.
It`s crazy; it`s a dream!

'My Mum and Dad?' They`re proud of me.
'My boy friend?' He`s called Keith.
'Credit crunch?' No bloody fear;
It ruins all your teeth.

'My social life?' Ah, well – no – yes.
Well, really, that depends.
Me and all my lovers are
The very best of friends.

'Am I happy?' `Course I am.
I`m famous, aren`t I? So –
It`s all fantastic, kindoflike.
'Contented?' Yeah – well, no. . . .

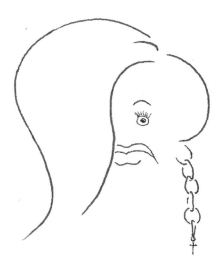

' ' Ow the ' ell should I know?'

The Nostalgist

On Christmas night I gaze into the fire,
And see a hundred patterns in the flame.
At times like this our fancies never tire
Of letting memories make us their game.

Drama flickers, light against the dark
Of blackened auditorium around.
The hiss and spit, the nudge, the soaring spark
Create a theatre of sight and sound.

And on that stage we re-create a past
Of hopes and triumphs, failures, and tears.
There act upon it the entire cast
Of characters from all our span of years.

How sharp they are, how magical, how strong,
These genies from the bottle of the mind.
How siren-like their story and their song,
How firm their urge to turn the eyes behind.

Look back; we see mistakes, regret, remorse.
Now look again; it`s love can bring relief.
Yet even when true love has run its course,
The price we pay for it, alas, is grief.

Now poke the coals, and change the words they say.
Our common sense must not be overridden.
The memories are aired. Put them away.
These treasures do not decompose when hidden.

We know the past is but a third of life;
The present and the future both blaze bright.
To make them ours, we must face doubt and strife.
We`ve *lived* the past; we own it as of right.

As hope, ambition carry us ahead,
The past has given us the strength to try.
Bereaved is he of whom it`s sadly said,
'He has no memories to make him cry.'

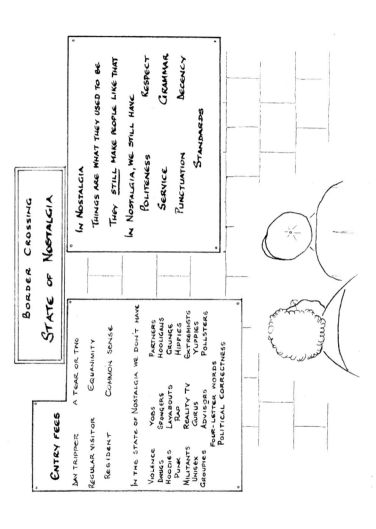

BORDER CROSSING
STATE OF NOSTALGIA

ENTRY FEES

DAY TRIPPER   A YEAR OR TWO

REGULAR VISITOR   EQUANIMITY

RESIDENT   COMMON SENSE

IN THE STATE OF NOSTALGIA WE DON'T HAVE

VIOLENCE	YOBS	PARTNERS
DRUGS	SPONGERS	HOOLIGANS
HOODIES	LAYABOUTS	GRUNGE
PUNK	RAP	HIPPIES
MILITANTS	REALITY TV	EXTREMISTS
UNISEX	GURUS	YUPPIES
GROUPIES	ADVISORS	POLLSTERS

FOUR-LETTER WORDS
POLITICAL CORRECTNESS

IN NOSTALGIA

THINGS ARE WHAT THEY USED TO BE

THEY <u>STILL</u> MAKE PEOPLE LIKE THAT

IN NOSTALGIA, WE STILL HAVE

POLITENESS	RESPECT
SERVICE	GRAMMAR
PUNCTUATION	DECENCY
	STANDARDS

'What do you think the catch is?'

The Carol-Singer

Plan the campaign round the corner;
Gather in the cul-de-sac.
Choose your target, let them have it –
'Hark the herald', front and back.

Joyful see the curtains rise.
Raise your chorus to the skies.
Hear the whispers through the door:
'Blast! It`s those damn kids once more.'

Our angelic voices say,
'Fifty p. – we`ll go away.'

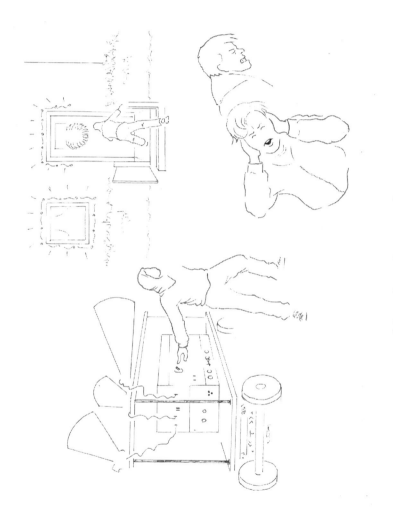

'4 - 3 - 2 - 1 - '

The Poet

My dream, each Christmas,
Is to write the definitive Ode.
If only my genius flowed
On the twenty-fifth of December,
The world would forever remember
This humble, sweating wordsmith at his forge of speech,
Whose aspiration is so far beyond his reach.

It certainly is not for want of trying,
Of praying, wishing, longing, or of sighing.
Both candle-ends and midnight oil are burned;
Rhyme after rhyme and verses neatly turned.

I`ve tried blank verse,
Both full and terse.
On gods` and Muses` heads I`ve poured my curse.

The Classics have been tried *ad infinitum* –
Alcaics, Sapphics, and hexameters.
You name the patterns, I have tried to write `em.
Free verse too – abandon all parameters.

Epic, limerick, ode, and sonnet –
Whatever tears I lavish on it,
Friends listen, and, in voice of ice,
Say, 'Charming. Oh, yes – very nice.'

No fringe group will print what I write,
No cranks or nerds or earnest greens,
No po-faced fundamentalists,
Or way-out, left-wing magazines.
No college offers to endorse
My poems for an Eng. Lit. course.

I've decided it's not that I don't write with sufficient unction;
It's that my family doesn't suffer from enough dysfunction.

I'm not consumptive, drunk, or high;
I'm not dead either, which is why
I'll never make it till I die.
Or truth -
In sooth -
That all, save me, have understood:
Perhaps I'm just not very good.

'You mean you actually understand them?'

The Agnostic

Just think about it: what's the legend worth –
The shepherds, mangers, wise men, virgin birth?
Consider each part purely as itself:
Have any of them made a better earth?

Believers say the further that one goes
In prayer and faith, the more God's power shows.
All very well. That's their belief, not ours.
'God knows,' they say, but we don't *know* God knows.

'The Bible will repay the time you spend.
Read on and learn,' believers recommend.
Again, it's only what some *others* say.
Page references to God can't be the end.

What do we really *know*, when all is done?
That life is short; its end shows death has won.
Why worry what awaits us past the grave?
How many have come back to tell us? None.

But what if God is *really* there – what then?
Divinity remains beyond our ken.
We have a life to live and nothing more,
And we must live that life among mere men.

If God exists, and merciful, we`re blessed.
We hope we have not from His path digressed.
If God is *not* there, well, that`s just too bad.
Our self-respect still says we do our best.

We try to show we`re good in what we do.
So let us carry Christmas all year through.
Faith, hope, and charity are God`s three tests.
We get by, mostly, just by passing two.

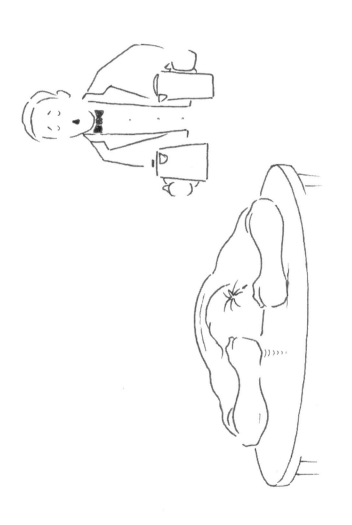

'Tea or coffee, sir?'
'I don´t know. I don´t know!!'

Rudolf

My name isn`t really Rudolf;
It`s Alexei Pavel Ivan.
But lyricists gave up trying
To make the damn thing rhyme or scan.

I don`t have a red nose either.
The others never called me names.
And I`d not be seen dead playing
Any of their soppy games.

How come then the story grew
About our Christmas Eve?
Truth about Siberia
People find hard to believe.

Tundra nights are cold and gloomy,
Till the Northern Lights appear.
Noses glow wet and rheumy –
Make the way ahead so clear.

But how could you write a lyric,
Tell the truth, and make it rhyme?
Aurora Borealis?
Such a feat would be sublime.

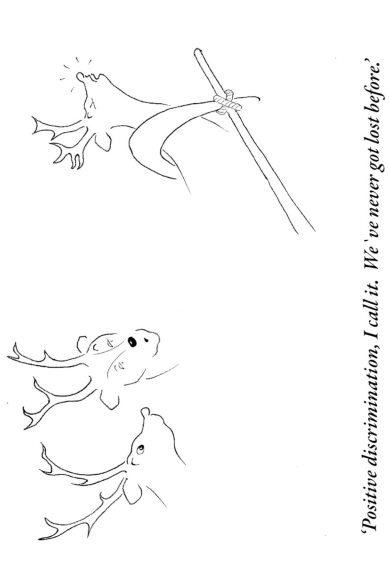

'Positive discrimination, I call it. We've never got lost before.'

The Boffin

You see us, clad in brown or white, drift vaguely round the place,
With clipboard in the hand and vacant looks upon the face.
We peer at dials and twiddle knobs and make our worried notes
With pens paraded in the top-left pockets of our coats.

Our work is very hush-hush, and we've signed the Secrets Act.
The Cabinet and Parliament don't know a single fact.
Our projects are not understood by any man alive,
And no-one even knows that we exist but MI5.

We do our dark experiments in Nissen huts on moors,
And crystallise our findings in debates behind closed doors.
Such journalists with telescopes as watch us from afar
Are scooped up by the Special Branch inside an unmarked car.

Yet every facet of the nation's life is touched by us,
From the tinfoil contraceptive to the under-water bus,
From rocket-powered fountain pens to sugar-candy glue.
The everlasting whisky flask? Oh, yes, we did that too.

Our Christmas project for this year – and we think it's a winner –
Is finding cheaper ways of laying on a Christmas dinner.
The plastic turkey bastes itself; injected with the taste,
It's soluble in gravy granules, so there is no waste.

Vegetables from old milk bottles – boiled or baked or fried.
Condiments from paper bags are easily supplied.
Christmas pud from cathode tubes, polystyrene pies –
Every marvel that a boffin brainstorm can devise.

Cream distilled from sump-oil – an imaginative source.
Wine from female ferrets` wee – matured in oak of course.
Follow our advice: you`ll make some very happy boffins.
If things go wrong, we also do nice artificial coffins.

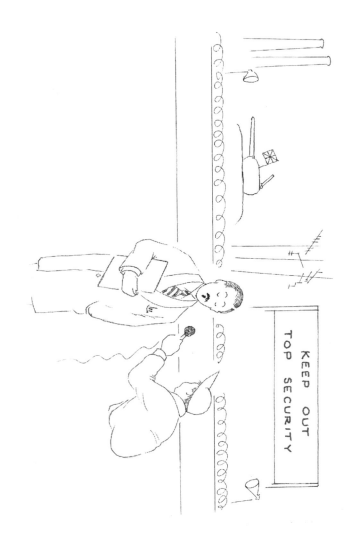

'This pill you've just produced. What does it do?'
'It simplifies our thought processes.'

The Stable Boy

It`s sixty years ago now, though it might have been last week,
The picture is so sharp and crystal clear.
I have a lot of memories, but this one is unique –
So unexpected, like, and – well, so queer.

You`d think a stable boy does lots of boring things all day
To do with mucking out and changing straw.
And normally I would agree – you`re right in what you say.
But then you didn`t see the things I saw.

The first thing I remember was a feeling of surprise –
What business had they being there at all?
And next I felt, like, curious, `cos there, before my eyes,
They made up beds beside a donkey`s stall.

And then I saw how big she was – and heavy. I thought, 'Crumbs!
She looks as if she`s very nearly due.
Suppose before my turn of duty ends the baby comes!'
I started feeling sick – well, wouldn`t you?

You`ll not believe the things he got me doing when it came.
At first I thought I`d pass out in sheer fright.
I sweated, and I blushed, and thought I`d die from very shame.
I tell you, I grew up in just one night.

But when it all was over and he turned to me and said,
'You choose the name; it`s only right and proper,'
I said the first damn stupid thing that came into my head . . . .
'Jesus?' she said. 'That`s fine.' I couldn`t stop her.

'Well, yes, Joseph helped a bit, but it was mostly me.'

The Politician

Friends, countrypersons, snug before your fire,
In every city and in every shire,
Give us your ears, and let us take the chance
To cast across our policies a glance.
That's why the face you now see on your screen
Is me, and not Her Majesty the Queen.
I'll prove, so every viewer understands,
Our country could not be in better hands.

We don't believe in running down the others;
As public servants, we and they are brothers.
They even make an effort now and then,
And don't forget they're honourable men.
We had to suffer thirteen wasted years –
Frustration, folly, toil and sweat and tears.
But why go through their record once again?
I must repeat: they're honourable men.
I'd rather still my tongue and break my pen
Than I would wrong such honourable men.

And thus you see our policies are sound.
We'll seize the reins and pull the country round.
So do not heed their silky siren song;
They may be honourable, but they're wrong.
May God be with you, whether He or She.
A Happy Christmas, and please vote for me.
I promise you, with me in Number Ten,
We'll have no need of honourable men.

'Take a card — any card.'

The Historian

Facts, facts, facts.
Test them – only strictest rules of evidence.
Axe, axe, axe.
Never grind it – equally strict tolerance.

Acts, Acts, Acts (and Gospels).
For objectivity, poor substitution.
Tracts, tracts, tracts.
Preaching to converted – no solution.

Alas, alas, alack!
A lack indeed of verifiability.
Alack, alack, alas!
A total absence of reliability.

Rack, rack, rack.
Place historians all unwilling on it.
Attack, attack, attack
Their pride in having no bees in their bonnet.

Back, back, back
They fall from making judgment – and their plea?
'I`m sorry – not my period, you see.'

'Damn the evidence! I just hate their guts!'

The Postman

[Until twenty or thirty years ago – or was it more? - it was customary for the last delivery of the Christmas post to arrive on Christmas morning itself. Many a postman found recipients, imbued with the festive spirit, unwontedly hospitable and generous. And until not so very long ago, postmen began their rounds very early in the morning, which meant that they had to get to their sorting offices even earlier.]

In the bleak midwinter, hours before the sun,
Nose and finger blue with cold, postbag weighs a ton.
Through the early morning gloom, everything is grey.
Spirits fall and shadows loom – God! It`s Christmas Day.

The holly and the berries enliven every door.
But letter boxes full of edges still can make your fingers sore.
Then lights go on in windows and shouts come from the hall.
The frost inside you starts to melt and you don`t feel quite so small.

Everyone likes getting the post; we`re the one they like to see most.
Rise the morning, fellowship dawning – come and share tea and toast.
Merry Christmas, Happy New Year. Eight, nine, ten, it`s just as sincere.
Beer and sherry, cider and perry, we`ve got a small cask of it here.

A dash of gin to lighten your load; a splash of Scotch, no less than
you`re owed.
Festive season, what better reason? Another one for the road. . . .

Oh, come all ye faithful, come and greet your postman.
The world is such a lovely place, I`ve never felt so good.
Come get your letters; I`ve got them down here somewhere. . . .
Down inside this lovely sack. . . .
How did I end up on my back?
Who the?. . . . What the?. . . . Lost the track. . . .
Woss the time?

William Shakespeare

As Yuletide looms, I shall, methinks, to Stratford go to play.
I had as lief not, as it might, for sure.
And spend some time with my good wife, Ann (lately Hathaway),
Less shrewish, hope I, than she was before.

For all that, it affords a change from precious theatre folk –
Escape, say I, as `twere not thus, `tis true.
I`m fed up with explaining every pun and every joke
To actors with a juvenile IQ.

Before my hearth, while logs do blaze, and beef is basted brown,
And greasy Joan doth keel a greasy pot,
I have a chance to chase my thoughts (and maybe nail `em down),
That flutter willy-nill through wit and wot.

I`ve read this book on Venice, which, for background, is quite new...
I`ve always fancied big scenes in a court.
Suppose I try to make the central character a Jew?
And he is backed by law! Now there`s a thought.

I scribbled down three words which had occurred to me one night –
'Friends, yeomen, countrymen!' They had a ring.
They might fit in a drama of Wat Tyler`s noble fight
Against the poll tax and his boyish king.

Then there was 'if music be the food of love, play on'.
I got that in some poxy Southwark stew.
I`d have King Richard shouting it from prison, whereupon
The minstrel Blondel his conclusion drew.

The oddest phrase that haunted me I`d jotted scores of times –
'To be or not to be' I wrote once more.
It didn`t seem to have potential in blank verse or rhymes.
And as soliloquy – a mighty bore.

I`d better stick to Venus and Adonis out of breath.
I can`t see future schoolboys liking plays.
It`s more fun reading poor Lucretia`s fate far worse than death,
Or seeing if seduction, like crime, pays.

'If you did something practical to help on a day like this. . . . .'

Joseph

Think of all the pictures that you`ve seen about that night.
You have to peer quite hard before you find me.
I`m the quiet figure, at the back, in feeble light.
No animal or person seems to mind me.

Not a single artist, though, has ever dared to leave me out.
Politically incorrect, of course.
Mary minus husband would have raised a wicked doubt:
Had Joseph left to sue her for divorce?

Nothing, I must tell you, could be further from the truth.
My age was something else they all got wrong.
Every version I`ve seen has me longish in the tooth,
Whereas in fact I was both fit and strong.

Everybody has their own opinion of me too.
So thick and fast the epithets have flown.
'Cuckold.' 'Softie.' 'Doormat.' 'Cipher.' 'He who never knew.'
But I know what I know. I cast no stone.

I can live with all the world misunderstanding me.
I never, thanks to one joke, get despondent.
Any time I like I can present a legal plea,
And summon God to court as co-respondent.

'Who are you, sir?'
'Joseph.'
'What do you do around here?'

The Drama Critic

Once I wrote my piece for the quality –
Times, Observer, Telegraph, Guardian.
The whole profession quailed before me –
Actors and managers, impresarios.

My opinion counted for everything.
All I wrote was pondered and analysed.
Careers and lives hung on my verdict –
Newcomers, juveniles, stars, and veterans.

Trends and movements, crazes and novelties,
Major breakthroughs – I spotted all of them.
My wit and style and waspish humour
Dazzled, delighted, diverted everyone.

I've seen all the best of the superstars –
John and Ralph and Larry and Vivien.
Not one today can match their talent.
Acting today is a mediocrity.

Speaking, writing, staging, and scenery
All show lack of originality.
In short, I'm forced to one conclusion:
Nothing I see now is what it used to be.

In my opinion, columnists, editors,
All have lost their taste and perceptiveness.
Of recent years they less employ me,
Turning down work of mine they once fell upon.

Well, if that's the way that the weather blows,
I'll retire and cosset my grievances.
The local paper will respect me.
Surely they'll print my piece on their pantomime.

'I see it as a major breakthrough.'

The Philosopher

Of course it all depends
On concepts, means, and ends.
Is reality the real, or just illusion?
Or is mere contemplation
The true illumination,
Without which simple vision is confusion.

For something to exist,
Must we first perceive the gist?
If we don`t see it, then it isn`t there.
But how can we conceive
A thing we don`t believe?
(A chance is here, I sense, to split a hair.)

Do scriptures yield their meaning
To our relentless gleaning,
Or are they traps God placed there to deceive us?
If all is so uncertain,
Do we simply draw the curtain?
But if we do not speak, where does that leave us?

'Of course the most important question is: "What is the question?" '

The Choirboys

Ring out the church bells, ding-dong dingle!
We make the carols go with a swingle.
We make the vicar glad he`s single.
Three little choirboys we.

Christmas should be a source of fun.
Right through the service we spare no one.
Every old caper under the sun.
Three little choirboys we.

Three little angels in the choir
Causing the organist to perspire,
Lining his stool with a naked wire –
Three little choirboys we.

One little choirboy sings the line.
Next little choirboy – descant – fine.
Third little boy makes an obscene sign –
Cute little cherubs we.

'Nowell' gives us a good idea –
Sing rude words, but not quite clear.
Vicar`s half deaf, so he can`t hear –
Dear little angels we.

Queer the pitch and spoil the metre.
Drink communion wine by the litre.
Shock and scandalise St. Peter –
Three Christmas angels we.

Encore

Let off a stink-bomb, cause sensation.
Verger faints with consternation.
Shock the entire congregation.
Things couldn`t better be.

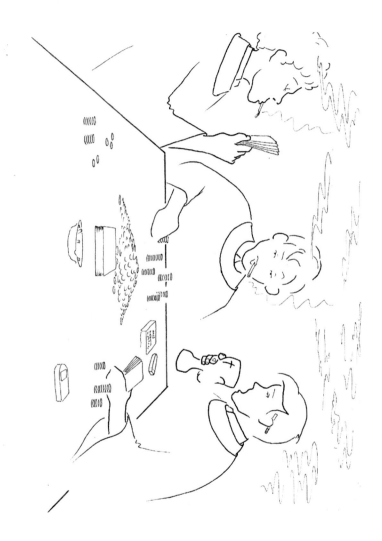

'I'll raise you five.'

James Bond

As I broke the bank with my last Swiss franc
(And I never turned a hair),
You could see the villain glare.
Then he fixed me with a stare:
'Mr. Bond, I see the die is cast;
I suggest you spend it mighty fast.
It`ll be your swansong in the Secret Service.'

But he didn`t know I was booked to go
To destroy his satellite
And his rocket-launching site
With my pocket-powered kite.
To the stratosphere I flew next day,
With a brisk seduction on the way,
And succeeded, with no crease in my tuxedo.

Now a grateful Queen so fit has seen
As to grant an MBE
To her servant, I feel free
To seek festive company;
I look forward to the turkey roast
On a sun-drenched opulent private coast,
As I shake, not stir, my vodka and martini.

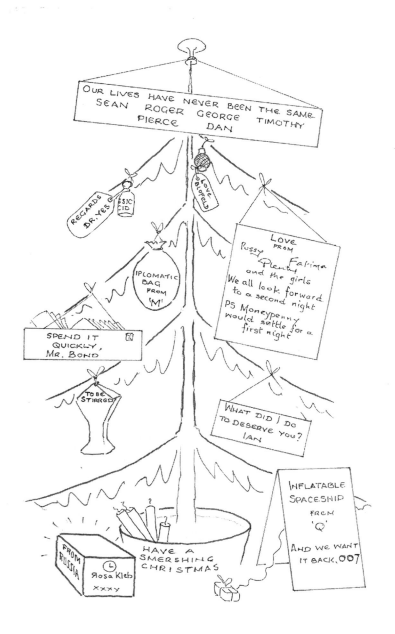

The Third Wise Man

I don`t think we`d have started if we`d known what was in store –
Desert, camels – burnt or freezing – everything so sore.
You`d think three men of our age would have worked it out before.
Makes you wonder why they call us `Three Wise Men`.

We simply got inquisitive about a piece of news –
About a king – a new one – that funny lot – the Jews.
The other two were all for going – how could I refuse?
We called ourselves `Three Kings`, not `Three Wise Men`.

The story-tellers got it wrong – I expect you must have guessed.
The famous star that guided us throughout our weary quest
Towards the state of Israel was in fact set in the *West*.
We came from the East, we Three Wise Men.

King Herod heard about our trip, and gave us board and bed.
Keen to worship this new king himself, or so he said.
I got the clear impression he would rather see him dead.
We weren`t born yesterday, we Three Wise Men.

We found this king at last, although we got a big surprise.
Cows and sheep? A manger? We could not believe our eyes.
A king born in a stable? It must be some disguise.
For a moment we were fooled, we Three Wise Men.

It was a bit embarrassing because of course we thought
Our destination was to be some posh, expensive court.
All the same we thought we`d better give him what we`d brought.
We didn`t have much choice, we Three Wise Men.

It wasn't very suitable when all was said and done.
A kid can't play with frankincense, and myrrh is not much fun.
But gold is not a bad investment in the longest run.
Perhaps we did him proud for Three Wise Men.

For our return, we thought another route was just as well.
By staying out of Herod's way, we wouldn't have to tell.
I think it was quite lucky, in the light of what befell.
Perhaps that's why they call us 'Three Wise Men'.

As years went by we thought about this business more and more.
He never got to be a king, or we'd have heard, for sure.
I wonder what became of him – that baby in the straw.
We like to think we were 'His Three Wise Men'.

The Ex-pat

Why stay on in England,
Bowed with cost and care?
Whoever breaks with England
Will soon become aware –
Of the autumn sun and the evening cup.
(England`s finished, all washed up.)
The truth hangs thick on the olive bough.
Come join us – now.

And after autumn, Noël follows.
In our cricket club, they`re all good fellows.
We roast the turkey, wolf the Christmas pud,
Play a game of snooker, maybe darts.
We tell ourselves it`s never been so good;
Whatever else we have no broken hearts.
Don`t ever think that we regret or grieve
Our first resolve to leave.

Although we don`t speak French, and don`t much try,
We shout and wave our arms, and we get by.
We`re getting old, but look at what we`ve got.
I tell you, England`s finished, but we`re not.

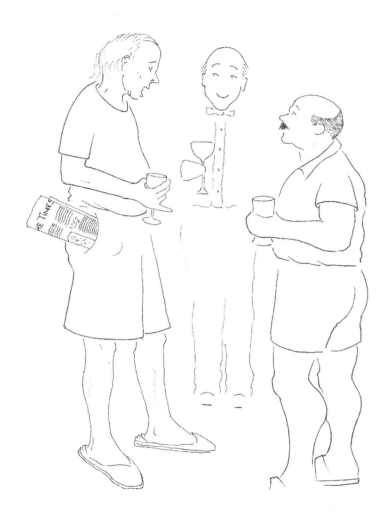

'I think we represent the best of remaining British values.'

The Atheist

Each year the same old charade is acted out.
Truth, reason, logic, and the brain are put to rout.
Nauseating fables,
Virgin births in stables.
Sane men surrender their capacity for doubt.

Hopes that these fairy tales will save the world are vain.
Two thousand years of hope have not removed the pain.
Science still rejected,
Miracles expected.
Thank God my atheism always keeps me sane.

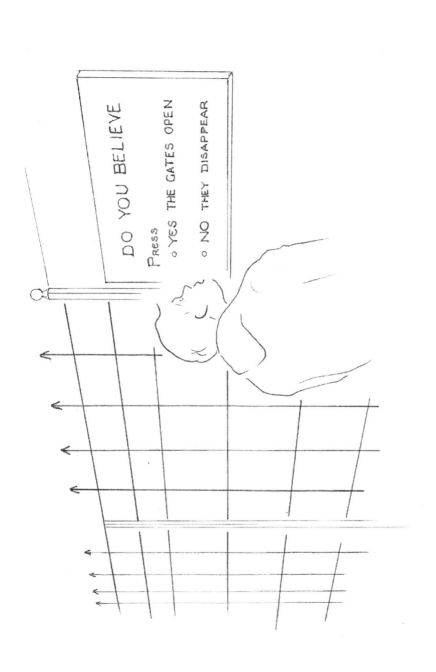

The Schoolboy

Apparently the Jews all saw it coming;
They`d known about it for a thousand years.
They`d had this chap Isaiah foretelling the Messiah:
King of all the earth, from what one hears.

Fast forward to the year of BC nothing –
Julius Caesar suddenly declared,
'I want the registration of the whole damn population.
In short, I want a Sensuous prepared.'

So this chap Joseph had to go to David.
'He has a house in Bethlehem,' he said.
But David let them down, cos when they reached the town,
They had to use a manger for a bed.

Then Joseph`s wife she went and had a baby.
She wrapped him up and laid him in the straw.
This was a little scary, cos Joseph and his Mary
Had never actually – you know – before.

The Bible says the culprit was an angel
Who flew in one day with the morning post.
He gave the startling news, which Mary daren`t refuse,
That she`d get preggers by the Holy Ghost.

I don`t find this consistent of the Bible.
It prints long lists of names – complete recall –
'Begatten' and 'begotten' (no-one is forgotten),
But Jesus came without 'begats' at all.

Then three men by the funny name of Maggy
Brought mere – whatever that is –and some gold,
And scent that they`d acquired from Frank (whom they admired?) –
An odd assortment if the truth be told.

Donkeys knelt and angels sang and shepherds stood and wondered,
And stars and Holy Spirits hung about.
Each person had a role, except for one poor soul:
Did Joseph feel a little bit left out?

Mr Chips

The poker lies astride the grate,
The toasting fork beside it.
A coal has burnt the rug again.
I haven`t tried to hide it.

Mrs. Wickett, my home help,
Is bound to click her tongue.
She hasn`t changed in fifty years;
She fussed when she was young.

Another friend has just gone home,
Who came to give me greeting.
We talked of old times, this and that.
We both felt good for meeting.

Although the room`s now empty, still,
With just the fireplace living,
To me it`s full of happy faces,
Laughing, loving, giving.

Two-three deep on the mantelpiece,
And all the other shelves,
Old pupils` cards, from each decade –
Grandparents some themselves.

The mystery is what I did;
I only taught them Latin.
What *did* they get from those dry books,
And those hard desks they sat in?

They didn`t speak it in their work,
Nor use it in their fun.
How many donned professors` gowns?
I`ll tell you truly – none.

I made no bones; it`s work, not games.
They`ll always see through lies.
Laugh, of course. Encourage – yes.
But don`t apologise.

A hard, unpleasant job well done –
You find that chord and strike it.
It doesn`t matter what you teach
So long as they don`t like it.

By some mysterious alchemy,
When all the Latin`s gone,
Something worthwhile may remain
To build a life upon.

Was my perspective limited?
Was I just half alive?
I married late, was widowed soon.
Nor did the child survive.

But I discovered love had stayed,
Unbidden, as it found me.
Maybe *that* is what I gave
To those who were around me.

So, when all is said and done,
I`ve had my share of joys.
It`s quite a family I`ve raised.
And d`you know what? – all boys.

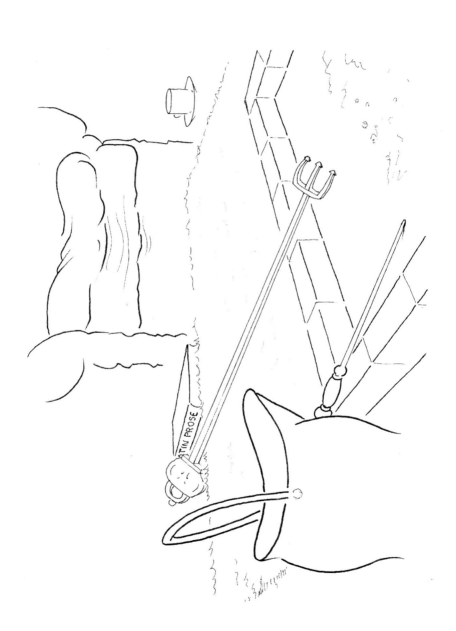

The Angel

Although I brought the First Nowell,
With wings and harp-strings thrumming,
In actual fact (the truth to tell)
I didn`t see it coming.

If you remember, I`d been sent,
About nine months before,
To tell this woman God`s intent,
And what she had in store.

It isn`t every day you tell
A piece of news like that.
This Mary took it very well:
She sang 'Magnificat'.

So that was that, and I forgot
This most unusual mother.
Well, I`m a busy angel, what
With one thing and another.

Then one day God gave out the word:
'Look sharp! Unfurl the banners!'
'What – now?' we said. He said, 'You heard:
Start practising hosannas.'

For what seemed weeks we sang away
To try and pacify Him.
'Again! Again!' was all He`d say.
We couldn`t satisfy Him.

Expectant fathers always make
An awful lot of fuss.
We smiled to see that God could take
On human cares like us.

So this was clearly going to be
A unique choral feast.
And who would come to hear and see?
Some emperors at least.

I always say you live and learn –
And you must take my word –
For, when we came to do our turn,
Only shepherds heard.

The Man in the Doorway

You ask how I see Christmas.
A marble step more brightly glowing,
More ankles and umbrellas going
In and out past windows showing
All that makes it gay.
Those that pass press nose on pane,
Can go and buy and leave again.
We sit here always, gaze in vain –
A sheet of glass away.

No memories to warm us?
It wasn`t always like this, no.
Times were better years ago.
But thinking only makes you low.
The memory`s a curse.
The 'then' makes 'now' a harsher fate,
And past is pain to contemplate.
The 'now' makes 'then' a joy to hate;
I don`t know which is worse.

No hopes then for the future?
Perhaps a warmer sleeping bag,
A coat that doesn`t look a rag,
Fresh cardboard, soup, another fag.
You criticise the choice?
Hopes need vision, vision height,
Height support to aid the fight.
We are so low we have no sight.
We have no help or voice.

The Primary Teacher

Hark the herald angels sing –
Village bells and ding-dong-ding.
Be prepared for anything.
All right on the night.

Secret of a good Nativity –
Maximum of child activity.
Never mind the sensitivity;
Get the balance right.

Casting problems from the start:
'Please explain,' coos Mrs. Hart.
'Kevin has no speaking part.
Can`t you see he`s bright?'

Sets, thank God, are not your care.
'Mr. Jenks can help you there.
He`s a handyman.' Beware!
Last year he fused the light.

Practice after school each day.
Always *somebody* away.
'Sandra`s ballet school today.'
'Will she come?' 'She might.'

Tears and tantrums, wear and care.
Joseph, tempted by a dare,
Pulls the Virgin Mary`s hair –
Naughty Israelite!

Costumes all make do and mend.
Truss them up and let`s pretend.
It won`t matter in the end.
Everything`s a sight.

Home-made curtains open wide.
Mums and Dads all glow with pride.
No-one cares the donkeys cried.
All right on the night.

'How come Jesus had two dads?'
'That's nothing; I've had three.'

The Dictator

My people will remember the next 25th December,
When I announce My Plan on television.
Though I am so far above them, they will all see that I love them,
And appreciate my statesmanship and vision.

I shall promise, by St. Mary, that my Foreign Secretary
Will never bend the knee to East or West.
We shall not apologise when our opium exports rise;
We`ll give attractive terms if they invest.

Our tax laws will provide a delightful place to hide
For the foreign and the greedy stinking rich.
I`ll keep crime off the streets, and stop anti-tourist cheats,
By gun or rope - it doesn`t matter which.

I`ll open all my gaols, and accept what that entails,
So foreign states can take the opportunity
To hide threats to security (while claiming legal purity)
And torture them with absolute impunity.

To prove our deep traditions and our hatred of munitions,
Our flag will show a simple bow and arrow.
My wife will show her passion for contemporary fashion.
I`ve put my eldest son`s name down for Harrow.

We`re open to request from every spokesman of the West
To come and do a deal, no matter what.
To iron out division, to facilitate decision,
We help by laying on a flashy yacht.

We follow the tradition of a man in my position –
Cancel all elections, get some aid.
Give amnesty next Monday, shoot dissidents this Sunday,
And choose some offshore islands to invade.

Whatever I decree, my state police will see
That acquiescence follows everywhere.
My propaganda media and my website wikipedia
Will comfort everyone that I`m still there.

My nation will endorse me; their prayers and cheers will force me
To make myself their President for life.
I`m having new coins minted, upon which I`ll have printed
An image of me kissing my dear wife.

My people will remember every 25ᵗʰ December;
I`ve made it *my* official birthday too.
The consequence, in essence, is that, when they give their presents,
They`ll give the biggest one to you know who.

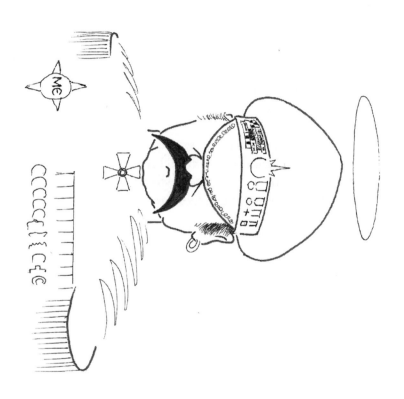

Sherlock Holmes

I see a frown on Holmes` face
Because he sees me lift my pen
To write about him once again;
He hates the way I dramatise.
No matter – here, for public eyes,
A rare unpublished case.

'Twas bitter cold, as I recall.
I had that evening turned my feet
To 221B, Baker Street,
To bring my friend some Christmas cheer.
We puffed our pipes and sipped some beer.
Then! – footsteps from the hall.

They stopped outside our stout oak door,
And Holmes threw me an eager glance.
'Perhaps at last there is a chance
Of using my deductive skill.
I`ve been so bored I`m almost ill.'
He leapt across the floor.

He pulled the door and gave a cry,
For there upon the threshold stood
A stout man in red coat and hood.
His beard was of a startling white.
His black belt was a trifle tight.
His boots came to the thigh.

'Who can it be?' cried I. Said he,
'How oft must I reiterate:
What can *not* be, eliminate.
Unlikely though it may appear,
You then have truth; the logic's clear.
It's elementary.'

He frowned, and stared. There was a pause.
'Your boots, sir, have peculiar toppings.
Observe them, Watson – reindeer droppings.
And see his coat – that line of grease.
Only sledge bars make that crease.
It must be Santa Claus.'

Our guest then gave a laugh so hearty
Holmes for once was lost for speech.
Santa Claus began to reach
To take his hood and beard away.
It was as much as I could say,
'Great Scott! It's Moriarty!'

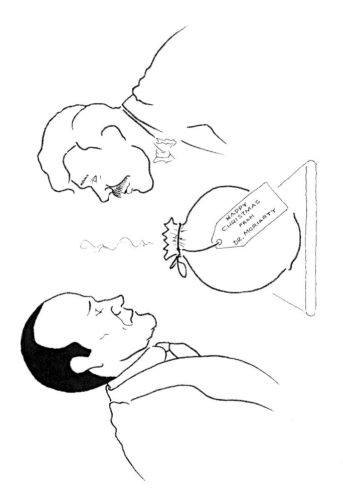

'You know my methods, Watson: observe and infer. What do you think it is?'

King Herod

They said they`d come to worship
A new-born King of the Jews.
My Counter-Terrorist Bureau
Had unearthed no such news.

An infantile usurper?
I`d like to see them try.
I killed the lot in self-defence.
King of the Jews – my eye!

'It was me or them. It's what they call raison d'état. If you were a king, you'd understand.'

The Martian

Report on Earth Reconnaissance – the Northern Hemisphere.
Facts observed quite near the ending of its stellar year:

Levels of technology – millennia behind.
State of evolution – they`re still stuck on mere mankind.
Planet preservation – they just haven`t got a clue.
Moral progress – altruism light years overdue.

But one odd thing was worth recording on our cosmophone:
Some furious activity throughout one night alone.
A man in red, upon a sled, came down from arctic climes,
And went down chimneys everywhere about a billion times.

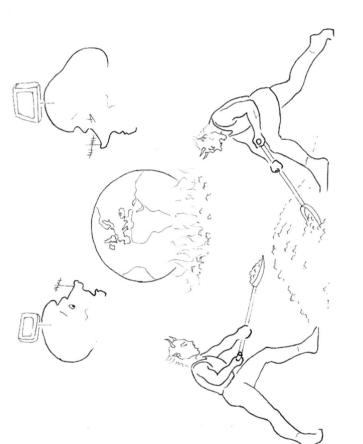

'I believe it is known as global warming.'

The Teenager

Whoever thought up Christmas?
A three-day, mindless, crushing bore.
Ghastly relations take over the house.
It`s worse than the Christmas before.

Politeness rules at Christmas,
Whatever aunts and uncles say –
Predictable clichés, embalmed in mould.
If only they`d all go away.

Babies swarm at Christmas.
How can cousins be so fecund?
One glance is enough for a sane, simple soul;
You certainly don`t need a second.

Put kids down at Christmas.
On purpose they will laugh and say things
To embarrass and tease. They`re deaf to your pleas.
They are beasts; you are simply their playthings.

Parents ruin Christmas.
Everything they do is wrong.
They haven`t a clue about anything *real.*
I ask myself, 'Do I belong?'

Much to do at Christmas.
Such bustle and business about me.
A hundred and one things that have to be done.
They`d never get through it without me.

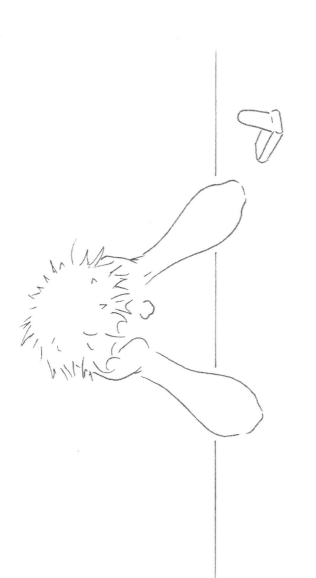

'Why doesn't anybody see?'

The Barfly

I wouldn`t have him in the house.
Prime Minister? The man`s a fool.
I say, d`you mind moving up?
I usually have that stool.

No. . . . politicians as a breed
Should all have been put down at birth –
The biggest, loudest, most deceitful
Gang of charlatans on earth.

Next time they make a cock-up, fine them.
That would teach `em, don`t you think?
I haven`t seen you here before. . . .
Oh, thank you. Mine`s a gin, please – pink.

The immigration rate`s gone mad.
For that alone they should resign.
God knows I`m not a racist, but
There comes a time to draw the line.

Now look at our appalling crime rate –
Murder, rape, and terror rife.
And when they`re caught, the law`s too soft.
I`d give `em all the rope or life.

The country`s going to the dogs –
The roads, the mines, the steel, the docks. . . .
Oh, yes, I live just up the road. . . .
The wife likes looking at the box.

The kids these days have no respect.
When we were young, we had to mind. . . .
One of each. I don`t know why;
When I come out, they stay behind.

If you ask me, there`s far too much
Of self and 'I' and 'damn you, Jack'. . . .
No, no-one tells me what to do,
What time to come out or go back. . . .

To Christmas lunch? Yes, when I`m ready.
Do I look like man or mouse? . . .
I must be off now. . . . What? Oh, no –
I wear the trousers in my house.

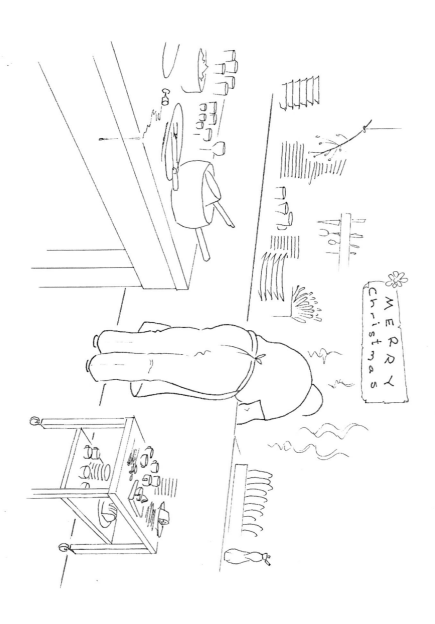

William the Conqueror

[An odd choice, this, for a Christmas anthology, but William was in fact crowned on Christmas Day, 1066, in Westminster Abbey. And crowned in what turned out to be circumstances of high drama.

When the time came for the congregation to show their acceptance of William as their King by raising a shout of acclamation, they duly did so, both Saxon and Norman. Because of the blending of their voices (and languages), the words were not intelligible to the soldiers on guard outside. Thinking that something had gone terribly wrong, they panicked, and began setting fire to houses nearby (which were of course made of wood).

When the smoke began to pour into the Abbey, the congregation panicked too, and rushed for the doors. Only a cluster of sweating bishops, chaplains, and monks remained before the altar. They rushed through the remainder of the service, with the new King himself, said one chronicler, 'being much alarmed'. (Most uncharacteristic of William.)]

At Hastings God decided my victory.
A frightened London offered me monarchy.
I took it, not ahead discerning
Westminster Abbey and Christmas burning.

[This verse is a short exercise in the Alcaic metre, a classic Greek device often employed by the Roman poet Horace, especially for portentous themes. Some translators of his Odes tried, and were able, to maintain the metre in their English versions.]

'I had it from my brother-in-law, who's chief candle-snuffer in the Abbey. It's William's coronation feast, and you know what their cooking's like.'

Mary

What do you expect me to say?
You know what I got involved in.
Could *you* contemplate it?
And if I *could* think about it,
How do you suggest I turn it into words?
Even if I did,
Would you believe me?

I can hear what all of you are thinking:
Why her? For Heaven's sake, why her?
How did it come about?
And why did she allow it all to happen?

I think you miss the point.
What actually *happened* is what matters.
No-one will understand the how and why.

Now let me ask you something:
If God had spoken to you, about *anything*,
Wouldn't you have gone along with it?

The Explorer

With Christmas nigh, spare one small thought for me,
Surviving in some distant foreign field
That we dress up as England. Wistful we,
Our sighs by camaraderie concealed.
And whether Arctic night or tropic glare,
We briefly tell ourselves we've ceased to roam.
We smell a winter fog or summer air;
However we imagine it, it's home.

If we love England so, why go away?
It's we love travel more, not England less.
We didn't choose it; it chose us; we're driven.
It's something we must do – not work, not play.
No madness, no obsession, nor mere stress –
A voice that drags us from our English heaven.

'I can't believe this: you forgot the cranberry sauce?'

The Particle Physicist

We don`t shout about it, we don`t advertise;
We don`t come on chat shows and chatter.
Yet if you knew our work, it would make you pop eyes.
We`re engaged on the Final Great Matter.

Yes, Newton and Darwin and Einstein were giants,
But we face a far bigger query:
Is it possible, out of all physical science,
To build a Grand Unified Theory?

Collect *all* the data (that is our dream),
And from this infinity draw
A simple, symmetrical, beautiful scheme –
The Ultimate Very First Law.

We don`t see much mileage in Jesus` birth,
Except as a reason for jollity.
It takes up more time and more thought than it`s worth.
You don`t find the Truth in frivolity.

You find it in neutrons and black holes and quarks,
In big bangs and space that is bent.
It`s never in Edens and Noahs and Arks,
Much less in the New Testament.

Now Science, God knows, is most unscientific;
Its rules are not written in stone.
Its dead ends are legion, its errors prolific,
But we still think Man works on his own.

There remains a great deal that we don`t comprehend,
And we cannot be sure we can do it.
We have to accept the faint chance, in the end,
That God might have beaten us to it.

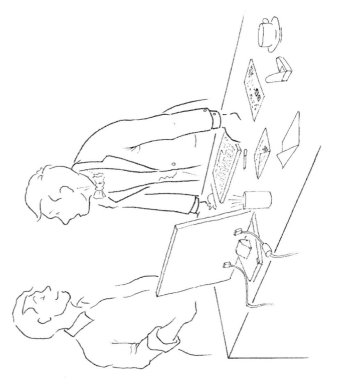

'And that's it?'

'That's it.'

The Old Maid

What I do, or I don`t do, at Christmas, my dear,
Is none of your business; it`s mine.
You are welcome to visit, if you feel the need.
If not, I assure you, I`m fine.

I`m healthy, I`m warm, I have plenty to do.
The hours are no burden to me.
Nor am I a burden to anyone else.
I don`t mind my own company.

I have friends; I have family; I love them all.
But I don`t want them here every day.
By the very same token, they don`t want me.
We are happy to leave it that way.

Of course I`m aware of what the world thinks,
And I know what their canny smiles mean.
They think they have worked out the person I am.
But they have no idea what I`ve been.

You cannot ordain what should happen to you.
You are thankful if Life is kind.
If it`s not, and it suddenly takes things away,
You make do with what`s left behind.

I`ve flattened a few blades of grass in my time.
The details are no matter here.
When he died, it was not that I gave up the search;
It`s just that I`ve not met his peer.

Charles Dickens

I`m a writer, presenter, reciter out loud,
Whose calling involves captivating a crowd
Of readers or listeners – matters it not,
So long as the drama is served to them hot.

Poverty, cruelty, poor house, or slum;
Richest of banquets, humblest of crumb;
Murderers, pickpockets, dandies, and fops;
Coaching-inn yards, curiosity shops;
Orphans and cripples, hypocrites, saints;
Anything seen by my mind my pen paints.
Virtue and evil, charity, crime –
All things appear on my pages in time.

The truth may be difficult, never unfair.
I write what I witness, whatever is there.
I add a good story, a laugh and a cry,
Good characters too - and I`m home and I`m dry.

But my greatest success, though I say it myself,
The one that made customers ransack each shelf,
Is the picture of Christmas - the bait on the hook -
That I drew on the pages of one little book.

Gas lamps and shadows, the fog and the frost;
Stamping and blowing, arms tightly crossed.
Fruiterers, poulterers, turkeys and roasts;
Faces in door-knockers, spirits and ghosts.
Mystery journeys, conscience and shame;
Crutches in corners, tears for the lame.
Window on morning, a glittering dawn;
Vows to amend, a man's soul reborn.

I season the mixture with holly and snow;
White breath on air and pink cheeks a-glow.
And presto! There's Christmas, as I have presented it.
Do I know about Christmas? Of course - I invented it.

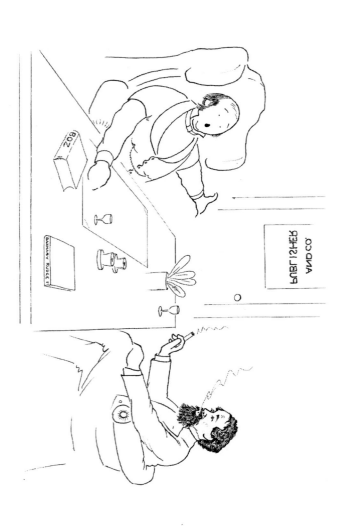

'A book purely about Christmas? Are you mad? You might as well write one about Candlemas or All Souls' Day. They'll never buy it.'

The Page

I work for Good King Wenceslas;
I`m what you call a page.
It may give me a touch of class,
But it don`t give me a wage.
An` what is worse, my king`s a saint –
Prayers, good works, an` all.
An` if you think that`s fun, it ain`t;
It drives you up the wall.

`E wants us all to be like `im.
We try, but it`s a trial.
I`m tellin` you, it`s bloomin` grim,
This life of self-denial.
All day `e`s spreadin` `oly light.
`E`s at it night-time, even.
What about that freezin` night?
When was it? . . . . Feast of Stephen.

We`d `ad an `eavy fall of snow.
The wind cut like a knife.
The temp`rature `ad dropped as low
As I`d seen all me life.
I was tucked up in me bed
(It`s lovely – full of feather),
When Wenceslas `e sticks `is head
Out just to see the weather.

`E sees this bloke collectin` wood
To put upon `is fire.
' `Ere`s a chance to do some good,'
`E says. 'I must inquire.
Just look at that poor chap. Dear! Dear!
Poor peasant! At `is age.
I wonder if `e lives round `ere.
I know; I`ll ask me page.'

So I was dragged from my warm bed
An` brought down in the `all.
' `Oo`s that bloke out there?' `e said.
'Where does `e live an` all?'
'Oh, Lord, not more good works,' I thought.
'Not this hour of the night.'
I blinked an` gave `im my report,
An` `oped it sounded right.

I said the furthest place I knew,
An` pointed to the east.
'St. Agnes, sir. Too far for you.
Three miles away at least.'
'That fountain place?' `e said. 'I know.
Come on.' So I replied,
'You can`t, sir, not in all this snow;
It`s freezing cold outside.'

'Tut-tut!' `e said. 'Of course we can.
Now go and get supplies.
We`ll take them all to that poor man,
An` give `im a surprise.'
`E saw the food and wine I brought
An` said, 'We`ll take logs too.'
*We`ll* take them! That`s a laugh, I thought.
`Oo carried `em? Guess `oo!

Ol` Wenceslas `e strode ahead
Like Jesus on the water.
I staggered after, like I said –
The overloaded porter.
A poet might have called the scene
'Frost-crystalled, silver-lacquered'.
Me? I can`t think when I`ve been
So absolutely knackered.

`E said, 'Step where I put my feet.
You`ll find it`s not so cold.'
It sounded daft, but I was beat;
I did as I was told.
Off `e went, with me in tow,
Bent over, puffin` `ard –
Covered `ead to foot in snow –
Jis` like some Christmas card.

I know you won`t believe this, but
What I`m so mad about –
When we reached this peasant`s `ut,
The bloomin` man was out.
Of course `e was – out gettin` wood.
It`s only common sense.
Y`see, though saints are very good,
They can be bloody dense.

'What is it – a Christmas card?'
'No, sire – my resignation.'

The Refugee

Christmas to us is a hut in a camp,
Or – if we`re unlucky – a tent,
While committees and agencies meet to discuss
Where the devil we`re all to be sent.

I know you don`t want us, but what could we do?
There was, simply, no other option.
When a child loses family, home, and support,
It must, perforce, canvass adoption.

For those who turned guns on us, bombs, or the gas,
Were clearly on homicide bent.
At least, if you only pretend we`re not there,
We`d die of neglect, not intent.

You make up your mind when you see us arrive,
Hollow-eyed, and cooped in a queue.
You decide we are shiftless, ignorant, crass –
Quite probably criminal too.

All we ask is a ration of space and of time,
To let us show willing to learn.
We are not all Albanian forgers and pimps;
We`re happy to work and to earn.

You`ve all enjoyed freedom for nine hundred years.
To us it`s a luxury – rare.
We don`t ask for privilege – only a chance.
We just want to breathe your air.

'Next!'

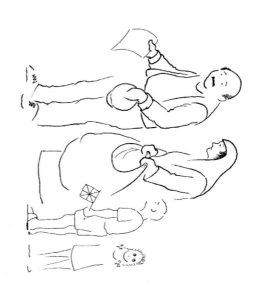

The Pensioner

The pub lost its licence a few years ago.
The post office too; they said business was slow.
The station, they told us, we'd have to forgo.
'You voted to put us in power, you know.'
We put up petitions; the answer was 'No!'
We sat and watched progress unfold.

We can't read the small print all over the place,
Computers now rule the entire human race.
It's all 'menus' now – not a voice, not a face.
The silicon chip has no charm and no grace.
The leisure of life has surrendered to pace,
And Christmas is feeling the cold.

I used to keep warm with a wife, and a son,
A daughter, some neighbours – good friends, every one,
A garden to potter in when the day's done,
A park to give Bonzo his evening run,
A cinema where all the films were good fun,
And life was so 'Lo and behold!'

The missis is gone, and the kids live abroad.
The air fare is something I cannot afford.
I sit in the cinema baffled and bored.
The only event I am glad to applaud
Is the fire in the flats on the park – thank the Lord –
Now a midden of rubble and mould.
(How Bonzo would love to have rolled.)

The veterans` club where we had a few beers
Is shut. They have all gone and died, it appears.
With regular funerals, no time for tears.
The interest rates do us no good, one hears.
My grandchildren haven`t seen Grandpa in years.
The car and the caravan? Sold.

The house had to go too; I live in a flat.
There`s no wall to lean on for gossip and chat.
There isn`t a back door to shake out a mat.
The tenancy rules say you can`t keep a cat.
We live in a world of the God Bureaucrat,
Whose statue is made out of gold.

Try telly for company – plays while you dine.
I heard better language up in the front line.
Of taste, class, and style there isn`t a sign.
The do-gooder army their efforts combine
To bring you *their* Christmas. It sure isn`t mine.
It`s hard not to scoff or to scold.

We were brought up to work and to stick to our ground,
To stay out of debt and to cherish a pound,
To try and be honest, reliable, sound.
Our age is no mystery, dark and profound;
We`re only young people who`ve just been around.
It`s you, never us, who say 'old'.

At Christmas I`m happy to see the fires lit,
But let me have my own opinions a bit.
The habits I`ve built up for years I can`t quit.
The life they now want you to lead makes you spit.
(The crimes that I`m tempted – dear God – to commit!)
They say I`m a bad-tempered, grumpy old git
Because I won`t do as I`m told.

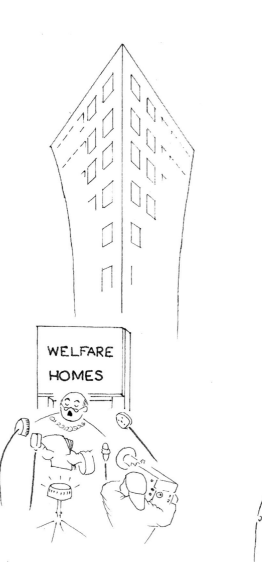

The Evacuee

'My dearest Dan, at last I can find time to sit and write.
So often, though, the trains run slow; I get home late each night.
Since this Blitz, we`ve had six hits on our part of the line.
You`ve no idea when things will clear. Last night it was gone nine.
I`ve heard from Dad. He`s very glad you`re safe out of the city.
He can`t get leave for Christmas Eve. I know; it`s such a pity.
I`m on call too. It`s hard for you. I did so want to come.
Please write and say that you`re OK. I miss you so. Love, Mum.'

The pencil hovers blind above the page.
The memory is bruised with scenes and words.
Three children of the family come first.
The toys were quick to go. 'We all share here.'
The sugar ration next. 'It goes for cake.'
One slice of bread allowed with jam – no more.
No bedtime story. No-one said goodnight.
Village school was worse – no playground peace.
London kids were very easy meat.
How to ease the growing ache of heart?
No home, no friend, no dog, no Mum or Dad.
No aunt, no gang, no secret place, no den.
A coach drove through with 'London' on the front.
It might as well have been upon the moon.

'Dear Mum, I know you can`t come, so I`m writing this to say
It`s all right here, and next week we`re all having Christmas Day.
Tell Dad I`m fine. He`s not to pine. And give my love to Gran.
I got your card. Don`t work too hard. That`s all, I think. Love, Dan.'

Ebenezer Scrooge

Christmas to me? Ooohh, Christmas to me
Was Fezziwig, hilly-ho, fiddle-dee-dee,
Party and pastry and pudding and pie,
Sun in the heart and star in the eye.
Shimmer on negus and bubble in beer –
Shyness evaporates, nerves disappear.
Blurring of fiddle-bow, rhythm and rhyme –
Mere standing sinful, sitting a crime.
Jigging and jogging and stomach-ache chords,
Flashing of shoe-buckles, echoing boards.
Sweatings and glowings and puffings and sighs,
Whooping and holleying, squealings and cries.
Sipping and nibbling in between measure,
Trapping in corner and stealing a pleasure.
Whispering, giggling, push in the chest,
Eyelashes lowered, thumbs in the vest.
Escape to the music, but keep up the chase –
A hundred emotions chase over the face.
Gambolling, tambolling, spinning and twirling,
Sporting and sparking and boying and girling.

Employer and guardian, carver of roast,
Leader of dances, proposer of toast
(Who swore he`d bring gaiety, proud of his boast),
Father and founder, magician and host –
You made it all happen, Fezziwig dear –
The holliest, jolliest night of the year.

Christmases nowadays? Just as much joy,
Thanks to young Fredrick, my late sister's boy –
Dear, delicate Fan, carried off by a breath.
Her love for us both makes a nonsense of death.
Her spirit continues in Fred's happy life,
In his house and his friends and his charming young wife.
They took this stiff bachelor in from the cold,
And he never felt silly or lonely or old.
I eat like a king at their dinners and teas;
I join in their games and their songs and their glees.
I'm partnered in dances and sat with on stairs;
I lose all my wrinkles and pains and grey hairs.
I have all the joy that can come to a man.
I owe all that joy to my dear, precious Fan.

Between my apprenticeship and my old age
There comes a hiatus, a gap, a blank page.
It's odd, but no memory comes back at all;
Not one of those Christmases can I recall.

'I've come to dinner, Fred.'

The Perfect Christmas Present

THE END

Lightning Source UK Ltd.
Milton Keynes UK
UKOW03f1053080114

224201UK00010B/310/P